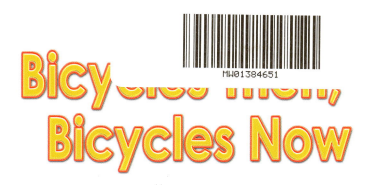

Bicycles Then, Bicycles Now

Diana Menefy

Contents

Learning Media

Bicycles Then

The first bicycle was made of wood.
It had two wheels and a bar.
Riders sat with one leg each side of the
bar and pushed the bicycle along
with their feet.
It was not very comfortable, but it was a
little faster than walking.

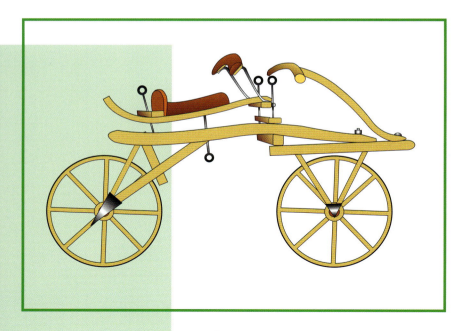

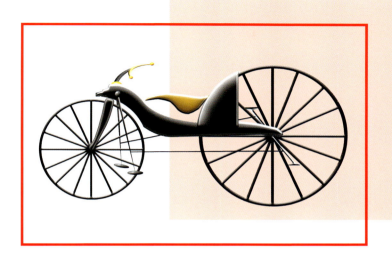

Pedals

Pedals were invented next.
The pedals went backward and forward
and pushed rods that turned
the back wheel.
This made riding bicycles a little faster
than before.

Soon, pedals that went around
instead of backward and forward
were invented.
Cranks turned the front wheel around.
This made a big difference.
Four years later, bicycles were being raced.

The High-wheeler

The High-wheeler was a different
sort of bicycle.
The large front wheel was chosen
to fit the length of the riders' legs.
These bicycles were also
called "penny-farthings."

Changes

Over the years, all sorts of changes
were made to bicycles.
Some bicycles had chains to make
the wheels go around.
There were bicycles with wheels
of equal size.
But all these bicycles
had solid rubber tires
on steel-rimmed wheels.
They were very bumpy to ride on.

A Big Change

Then John Dunlop invented a tire
that could be filled with air.
It was much more comfortable
for the rider, and it was
the last big change for many years.
Even the frame stayed
the same triangle shape.

Bicycles Now

Now, most bicycles have gears,
but they still look much the same
as they did many years ago.
It's the materials the bicycle is made from
that have changed.
Bicycles are now made from lighter and
stronger materials.
These bicycles are much more comfortable
than the old wooden bicycles were –
and they are much faster too.